WHEN DIGITAL DONE RIGHT

WHEN DIGITAL DONE RIGHT

LEADING DIGITAL TRANSFORMATION
IN THE PUBLIC SECTOR

RAPHAEL HUI

To Grace and Aloysius

CONTENTS

1

It Is Hard to Do Digital Right

"We must start the transformation now. If we stay at where we are today, it won't be long before the business abandons us completely."

I looked at our new CIO. She finished the presentation of her transformation vision with passion and a tone of finality.

And then, I looked at her direct reports in the workshop, the most experienced and senior IT leaders in TransCo. One or two of them seemed slightly uncomfortable, but most of them simply looked uninterested, just as I expected.

After all, Kate was already the third CIO of TransCo in the past three years. Her predecessor also wanted to change the world on his first day. Still, before he could make any fundamental changes, he abruptly resigned after only 14 months of reign, leaving the IT department essentially the same. These senior leaders were probably thinking, Kate had no idea how things worked here, and she was just trying to assert her authority. Perhaps a few of them might even believe that she would not be staying in her post for long? After all, she was the IT Director from a multinational investment bank with no experience in transportation or the public sector.

"Is there any question so far? I would like to hear your feedback." Kate asked politely.

"Thanks for your presentation, Kate," said Arthur, the Head of System Development. He was one of the most experienced engineers in the department, highly respected by the team and a solid contender to the CIO position. "I'm sure there is always room for improvement. But I still couldn't see the urgency for the transformation you proposed. After all, we have been doing okay all along...."

And he had a point: TransCo's IT department was one of the largest in-house software development houses in the region. They developed the MetroSys, one of the most advanced rail transportation management systems of its time. It automated many train operations and seamlessly integrated with engineering, asset management, and staff rostering systems. MetroSys played a critical role in the daily work of over 40,000 engineers, station managers, frontline operators, and management staff in TransCo. They supported the rail services for over 1 billion passengers every year. At the same time, TransCo's IT has been doing well with cost efficiency: the total development cost of MetroSys was only a fraction of the major vendor products.

"Also," Arthur continued, "I agree that our IT colleagues should update their technical skills. We can always invest more in training. But perhaps a major reorganisation is a bit too much? I am afraid it will cause staff grievances and may even risk losing our best people."

TransCo's IT had some of the most experienced rail transportation IT system design and development experts in the region. The team was dedicated and passionate about meeting their business users' needs. It had a low staff turnover compared to the industry average. Many staff members had been working in the department for over 20 years. Sure, TransCo paid them well and was a public organisation. As such, people might stay for stability. However, from what I saw, many of them carried a real sense of pride and purpose. They understood that they were not just writing software, but supporting the lifeline of the city.

"I am not quite sure about the innovation part, Kate," said Rex, the IT infrastructure department head. "You mentioned that you would like the team to explore emerging technology for the future. However, our team has been so busy with the projects at hand. We have committed a tight deadline to the Board and the government, you know. I don't know if we can cope with so much new stuff..."

"In fact, our CEO doesn't like innovation," Arthur interjected, "a few years ago, the CIO back then proposed to introduce robots for customer service at our train stations. The CEO then flatly dismissed the proposal and said that the media and the general public would go ballistic as to why we used public money to 'buy new tech toys'."

Kate seemed to be prepared. She put up another Powerpoint slide and said, "I know our team has done a great job so far, and I appreciated that. But I interviewed some of our key business stakeholders, and their feedback worried me."

"We had 11 severity-1 IT incidents in the past 12 months. In one case, twelve of the stations needed to fall back to manual ticketing operations for 3 hours. Haven't you seen the massive queue from the news? Don't tell me about big ideas. Can't you just make those incidents less frequent?" quoting one frontline station master.

"I have no idea why IT is so expensive, and when people say IT is becoming more important to TransCo, I am even more concerned." this quote came from one of the executives from the Finance Department.

"I can't understand why I need to wait for two years to entertain a simple system enhancement request." quipped an engineer.

The IT executives in the room started to look uneasy. And

then Kate showed the final one:

"I wish we could have an alternative to our in-house IT." this quote came from none other than the CEO himself.

Kate paused for a moment. Then she continued, "I understand you and your team have all been working hard. I am impressed that our projects are almost always delivered on time and within budget. But time has changed, and business is asking for more, even if they don't explicitly tell us so..."

"We knew that," it was Arthur again, his tone was getting a bit impatient, "we knew all of that."

"But with all due respect Kate, I think you might have overreacted a bit. The business always complained about something, even if we delivered almost all projects as they requested, on time and within budget. And we did. Also, even if they are unhappy with us, they have to stick with us anyway, aren't they?"

There was silence. Apparently, Kate did not expect such a direct rebuttal, especially in her first workshop with her direct reports. She sensed that her authority was being threatened, and, more importantly, her vision of transformation seemed to be at risk.

If you were Kate, what would you do?

What Makes Digital Transformation in the Public Sector So Difficult?

Digital transformation is inevitable for all organisations in every industry, especially after the COVID pandemic, forcing many business operations to go digital. This, of course, also applies to organisations in the public sector: many public services, from healthcare to education, need to go online, and remote working has become a norm under the "new normal". To fully embrace digital, however, organisations must go beyond technology, and in-depth change and realignment of process, mindset and culture are essential to make it last.

As any veteran change leader would know, it is never easy to transform a large organisation. However, it is even more difficult to transform an organisation from the public sector, where stability and prudence often trump disruption and innovation. But why is that the case?

This goes back to the fundamental nature of the public sector organisations. According to a report by the Economic Commission for Europe, United Nation, there are six major characteristics that define a public organisation. As you will see, every one of these characteristics poses specific challenges to digital transformation:

1. **Lack of competition**: Compared with private

enterprises where external and internal competitions are the norm, public sector organisations have very limited, if any, competition, both externally from the market and internally among staff. While this creates stability, it also means a lack of motivation or urges to transform and innovate.

2. **Need for openness**: In most democratic societies, the general public expects transparency and openness when it comes to the operations of public organisations. While this is important for maintaining a well-governed and fair system, it is challenging to hide plans of sensitive organisational change under heavy scrutiny, even if exposing it prematurely will create significant obstacles or even jeopardise the change initiatives.

3. **Constraint ability to act**: Agility is essential to digital transformation, where new ideas can be freely experimented with, adapted and evolved in short iterations with as little constraint as possible. However, with less autonomy than in the private enterprise, public sector organisations find it hard to be agile. They need to acquire explicit approval from various governance bodies for every action.

4. **Intolerance of failure**: Public sector organisations are entrusted and held accountable to make the best use of the public resources that they are allocated. It also means that any failure of initiatives, no matter big or small, could be perceived by the public as irresponsible

in using public resources. As setbacks and failures during digital transformation are common or even inevitable, this could pose a major problem.

5. **The difficulty of perceiving demand**: Public sector organisations typically do not face market competition like their private counterparts. This could result in being less sensitive to the demand and feedback from the external stakeholders. In addition, although they may need to justify the return on investment (ROI) of their investment, especially in recent years, the overall funding mechanism is still more driven by public policy direction and politics, rather than the business performance or outcome of previous investment. Therefore, there is less motivation to change in response to external drive or threat.

6. **The problem of institutional size**: Compared to private startups, public sector organisations are usually much more extensive in scale and staff strength. The sheer size of the organisation and the resulting diversity of internal stakeholders already make the promulgation and adoption of any new initiative much more difficult. It also means a higher chance of encountering issues such as silo teams and conflicting internal objectives and cultures, posing another layer of challenge to the transformation effort.

These do not mean that it is impossible to transform a public organisation digitally: instead, what you should do is to recognise the above constraints and strategise your transformation that aligns to, or at least minimises the conflict with, those constraints.

And this is where this book comes in.

What This Book Is About

I wrote this book because I understand how daunting it is to make digital transformation happen in public sector organisations. Having served as an advisor on digital strategy and transformation for both internal and external public sector clients over the past 15 years, I have seen both success and failure cases, and more importantly, learnt valuable lessons on how to do digital right in the public sector.

On the other hand, I always believe it is more meaningful and impactful to successfully transform a public organisation than a private company, as the outcome benefits not just the customers of a company but also all citizens. The sweat and toil of the transformation effort are not simply for financial gain but also for the public good.

As such, I would like to share some of these lessons learnt with you, as the CIO or senior IT leader from the public sector, who plan or is going through the same journey in your organisations. In this book, rather than talking about the digital technology itself (which is already discussed in many works of literature), I am going to focus on the process and people aspects of the digital transformation, and discuss the principles and approach for addressing the following three fundamental questions:

1. **Create a vision that works**: How to develop and communicate your vision of digital transformation that will win the buy-in of a diverse profile of stakeholders?

2. **Transform your team that performs**: How to transform the structure, people practice, behaviour and culture of a public organisation, in order to position your team to embrace your digital vision?

3. **Incubate innovation that matters**: How to introduce innovation and engage business and IT in a highly constrained corporate environment?

This book is divided into two parts: the first part (Chapters 2 to 4) describes the core framework and practical guide for addressing the three questions mentioned above. The second part (Chapters 5 to 7) builds on what presented in the first part and discusses what it takes to scale up and sustain the digital transformation effort.

While I understand every organisation is unique, the principles described in this book should still apply to most public sector organisations, regardless of their industry or jurisdiction.

Learning is a two-way process. While I hope you would find this short book inspiring for designing and executing your digital transformation journey, I am also eager to hear your feedback and learn from your experience as well. You may visit https://www.whendigitaldoneright.com/ to provide your comment and share your insight with me. Additional templates will also be available for free download on the website.

And now, without further ado, let our learning begin.

Part 1
The Fundamentals

2

Narrating Your Digital Vision

Just like you, almost every CIO has an aspiration that, one day, their enterprise IT organisation will become what the IT strategist Peter High described as "world-class IT" and will be regarded as such by their business counterparts. And just like you, they may also have a grand vision of digital transformation for their company that will automate its operation, revolutionise its ways of working, capture new business opportunities and deliver new values to its clients. As a CIO working for a public sector organisation, you may even aim to provide greater public good via technology and innovation and make your community a better place to live in.

So, let's say you were the new CIO of a public healthcare organisation, and you had a great idea that will help speed up the diagnostic process of certain chronic diseases. You identified a solution that harnessed the power of big data and applied artificial intelligence (AI) for medical imaging. To ensure optimal user experience, you decided that the answer would be building it in-house to optimally integrate with the current workflow of the doctors and nurses in the organisation.

You recognised that this would not be a trivial task. So you meticulously planned and crafted a multi-year roadmap to acquire the infrastructure, design and fine-tune the AI model with local clinical data set, develop and integrate the system, and source the talents required. After a month of preparation, you were ready to present your great idea and plan to the organisation's top executives.

Unfortunately, when you stepped into the boardroom, what was waiting for your passionate presentation was an uninterested group of business executives. The problem was, they did not think that you were addressing an issue that they cared about: sure, the population was aging, and their clinical frontline was facing an increasing service demand, but from your presentation, they only heard a lot of jargons and trendy technical terms, and counld not relate your idea to their workforce shortage problem.

Worse yet, when you started presenting your multi-year roadmap, the business executives bombarded you with many tough questions: What if the AI made a wrong diagnosis? Have you "socialised" your ideas with the clinical teams? Have you sought support from the dozens of task forces, user groups and governance in the organisation? Why did you need to ask for so many new headcounts? Why did it take so long and cost so much?

You tried to address their concerns, but no matter what you said, they only seemed to be more confused than before. Needless to say, you failed to get the board's support, and your idea stayed as, well, just an idea.

A year later, you were summoned to the same boardroom again. This time, though, instead of you selling a technology idea to them, they requested your team to deliver the AI solution that you lobbied for a year ago. The back story was that there were a few clinical incidents recently due to untimely reviews of the massive amount of X-ray images by the overworked doctors, which turned into a major public relations catastrophe. A few executives had heard from their industry peers about using AI to help to screen the clinical images at a fantastic speed. Therefore, they were now calling you in and said, "We should use AI in all of our hospitals and clinics as well. Can your team make it happen by the end of this year?"

You looked at them in disbelief, though you tried your best not to show it. For one thing, you could not believe that they had made a complete U-turn in one year just because of a few bad press coverage, and it seemed that they had completely forgotten it was you, not them, who first thought of applying AI in the organisation. Secondly, it was virtually impossible to get the job done in a few short months. Perhaps it was possible to conduct a product trial at one selected hospital, but a full-scale implementation with reliable technical infrastructure, AI model and the business workflow aligned to serve a few dozen hospitals, over a hundred clinics, and over a million cases per month (I forgot to mention that your organisation was the largest public healthcare provider in the region)? You know that it was almost destined to fail.

But whose fault was this? While the business executives seemed impulsive and unreasonable, unfortunately, it was you, as the CIO, who had to bear the major responsibility for the whole fiasco. It was because you might not be doing good enough as an enterprise CIO, whose key role was to serve as the bridge between IT and the business.

The CIO's Dilemma

Gartner defines the role of CIO as someone who oversees the IT people, processes and technology "to ensure they deliver outcomes that support the business's goals." I would take this a step further and argue that you, as a CIO, need to understand the needs and opportunities of the business proactively, and help them mitigate the gaps or capture the opportunities via IT service provision and product delivery. At the same time, you need to maintain effective communication with the business stakeholders to ensure that all parties are on the same page and are aligned with your objective: being "world-class".

It is easier said than done, though. Executive boardrooms of public sector organisations are usually not a place for new technology ideas. The things you might hear the most when you propose a new technology initiative would be "governance", "evidence that it works", "this is not the way we do things here", and if you are asking for funding, "why so expensive" - even when the investment you are asking for is insignificant compared with the daily business operating costs.

This is more often the case if you are lobbying for what I called the "technology backbone" investment, which typically covers technology infrastructure or platform development, such as networking, cloud infrastructure, or data platform. These initiatives are usually highly technical and often do not have apparent and immediate benefits to the business. Nonetheless, they provide essential technology capabilities indispensable for enabling future IT solutions and products, which will yield more direct and visible benefits to the business.

As a CIO, you may find this dilemma familiar to you: how to let the business agree to these technology backbone investments, so that you can realise **for them** the future business value that you know they will ask for one day?

You may think that the key is to let the business understand your point. After all, technology always sounds complex and scary to non-technical people. Therefore, many CIOs spend a lot of effort coming up with good analogies for explaining technical concepts in layman terms, and visualising the technical idea as much as possible. These are well-intended moves, but they are only the first step. My experience is that if you solely focus on educating technology to the business executives, they may either be uninterested in what you preach, or worse, leave the room with more questions and doubts than before.

Therefore, the first thing you need to keep in mind is: you are not here to be the IT professor of the executives; you are here to be their partner and advisor. Making the business executives understand the technical concept is one thing. Still, your primary objective is to secure their buy-in of your digital vision by persuading them that the vision is **relevant** and

matters to the business and them personally.

And it all comes down to you, the CIO, to package and communicate your digital vision and strategy, and help them realise the relevance of those strategies to themselves.

The Demand-Supply Framework for Narrating Digital Vision

To break the above dilemma, many CIOs tried to show the linkage of their digital vision with the overall business target or strategic directions when presenting to the business. While this could be helpful for straightforward initiatives (such as a new app or feature for a defined segment of customers), it would be trickier when you use this approach for more complex ideas that their business beneficiaries are difficult to define. Suppose you only link your digital vision to a high-level business mission or direction that does not have a clearly defined business owner (such as adopting cloud infrastructure for "better customer experience"). In that case, you will have a hard time securing support from any of the business executives.

Rather than linking your digital strategy to an abstract concept, a better way to approach this issue is to relate your digital vision around the need or "demand" of your stakeholders as persons, and then derive the technology infrastructure and services that "supply" the enabling capabilities to fulfil those needs. You will then form a much more cohesive narrative that naturally connects and aligns your vision to the business and better resonates with your audience.

The following "Demand-Supply Narrative Framework" can guide you through this process:

Step 1: Identify your digital stakeholders and analyse their persona

You first start with identifying the individuals or groups that are "relevant" to your digital vision, i.e. those who will be positively or negatively impacted during and after the realisation of the digital vision. You should also include those you will need their contribution to realise the strategy (such as your own IT staff) or need their buy-in and support for its successful realisation.

So who are your digital stakeholders? In private enterprises, it is usually more straightforward, with (broadly speaking) customers, competitors, suppliers and regulators externally, and business and IT internally. However, it can be more complex in the public sector. Depending on the reach and complexity of your vision, you may need to conduct a comprehensive 360-degree review that covers the following groups:

1. **IT Executives**: this group includes your direct reports and your senior IT management team, who will assist you in driving and leading the implementation of the vision.
2. **IT Frontline**: this group includes the supervisory and frontline IT staff, such as the middle management, the IT engineers, architects, analysts and other administrative and support teams. They will be your

main force to turn your vision into reality.

3. **Business Executives**: this group includes the top business management and governance bodies who are the key decision-makers of your organisation, such as the CEO, the top business executives and board members.

4. **Business Frontline**: this group includes the non-IT employees and team in your organisation from other business units, from middle management to the frontline staff. They are usually the major users of your IT systems and services. Still, more than that, they also play a crucial role in supporting and collaborating with

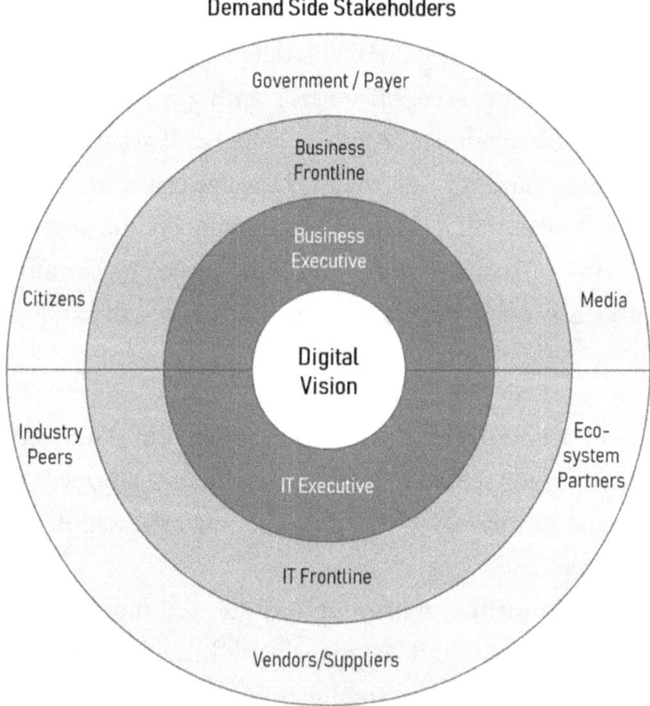

Figure 1 360-Degree View of Stakeholders

your IT team to realise your digital vision, and even serve as the evangelists of IT value.

5. **Government, Sponsors and the Public**: this group is, in a sense, the "boss" of your organisation, including the government agencies, oversight committees and governance bodies who have direct or indirect control of your organisation, or provide funding to it. It also includes your end users outside your organisations and, to a broader extent, all stakeholder groups external to your organisation that may influence, obstruct, or be impacted by your digital vision, such as the media, the unions, watchdog organisations, pressure groups, and other relevant segments of the general public.

6. **Suppliers, Partners and Peers**: this group of stakeholders directly provides the products, services, expertise, and advice to you and your IT team to strategise and deliver the digital capabilities required for your vision realisation. Vendors are probably the first ones you would think of in this group, but it can also include other partners in the technology or industry ecosystem, such as startup incubators, applied research institutions, Technology Transfer Offices (TTOs) from universities, think tanks, and even industry peers.

Once you have identified the relevant stakeholders, the next step is to perform an in-depth analysis of these stakeholders. There are three layers of understanding: the first one concerns the more superficial aspect of your stakeholders that are easier to be observed, including their capabilities or strength in supporting or contributing to the realisation of the digital vision (such as technical or domain expertise, financial prowess etc.), as well as the weakness or limitations they have that could potentially hinder their support to your vision.

The second layer is harder to discover: the intrinsic desire, fear, and emotion of your stakeholders. You should put yourself in your stakeholders' shoes, be empathetic to each of your stakeholders, and think of their personal needs, desires, concerns, distaste and fears. Try to understand what motivates them to support the digital transformation vision, and what may discourage them from doing so. This could be, for example, potential financial / resource / time commitment, change in process and practice, culture, or even shift in political power etc. As such, when performing your analysis, it is more preferred, where possible, to think of a "human with flesh and blood" rather than an abstract organisation or team.

The final layer concerns the external factors, such as business opportunities or threats, that may shape or influence

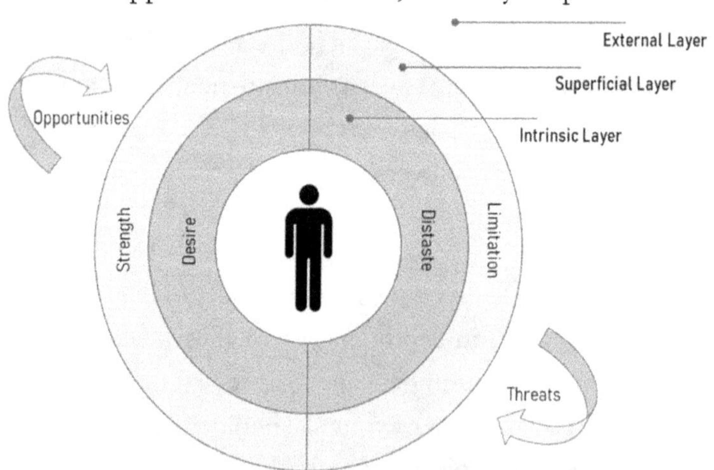

Figure 2 Three Layers of Stakeholder's Understanding

their opinions. These might seem trivial, but the challenge is to consider these from the perspective of the individual stakeholder, especially factoring in the superficial and intrinsic characteristics of the stakeholders. This way, you will be able to discover more accurately the opportunities and threats that they genuinely care about.

You do not need to go overly detailed for all identified stakeholders. In general, the more influence a particular stakeholder has over the implementation of the digital vision, the more thoroughly you should analyse them.

To aid your analysis process, you may construct a "user persona" of each of your stakeholder groups. This method was first adopted in the software design community, and is now a commonly used technique in marketing and User Experience (UX) design to represent the key characteristics, attitudes and behaviour of a group of users via an archetypical person. To design a user persona for your stakeholder groups, you may refer to several good templates, such as the Empathy Map Canvas by David Grey. Also, your organisation may have already performed a similar analysis when defining their overarching business strategy, which could help you jump-start this step. In any case, it is essential to validate your work with the corresponding stakeholders. Various customer research techniques, such as guided interviews or focus groups, could aid your discovery and validation process.

Step 2: Associate digital vision components with the stakeholders

After gaining a comprehensive understanding of your stakeholder, you can now build the digital portfolios by associating the components of your digital vision with the persona of those identified stakeholders, starting with those on the demand side. The demand side digital components usually refer to the product, services or initiatives that the IT team will provide or enable for the direct consumption of your stakeholders and can directly address their needs or support them to achieve their objectives. Examples may include new apps, devices, and services.

After constructing the demand side portfolio, the next step is to identify which capabilities in your digital vision must enable the components you have envisioned in the demand portfolio. These digital capabilities may include the technology infrastructure and platforms and any transformations required in architecture, process and practice, team structure, talent mix, and people behaviour or culture. You can discover and examine these capabilities by applying the Technology-Process-People framework against each of the major components in your demand-side portfolio:

Technology, such as:

- New technologies that are required for enabling the identified digital vision components
- Scaled-up or consolidated existing technologies or service provision for satisfying the projected business demand
- New (or significant scaled-up) major platforms and infrastructure required to support the new or

revamped technology provision

- New addition or change of existing tools for building and maintaining the other technology provisions

Process, such as:

- New technology policy and processes needed to support the expected function and volume of the identified components in the demand side portfolio
- Transformed / scaled-up existing processes in response to the new technology provision or expected exponential increased service demand
- New or updated key performance indicators (KPIs) and other metrics, as well as mechanisms for defining and tracking them, in order to measure new / revamped service targets, business outcome, or team / individual performance

People, such as:

- New skills and knowledge that will be required to develop and run the technologies and services identified in the demand side portfolio
- New or transformed organisational structure, as well as roles and responsibilities, skill mix, level of staffing and resource of individual teams for the effective delivery of the other components of the digital vision
- New ways of working, team norms, and individual's behaviours for the effective functioning of the organisation
- New or revamped mechanism for acquiring talents

- Mechanism or platform for networking and engaging with ecosystem partners

With these supply-side capabilities identified, you can then consider who among your supply-side stakeholders will be able to contribute to the realisation of those capabilities: it could be your frontline IT team who will develop the new apps and features; it could be your IT leadership team, who will drive the process and culture changes of your organisation; it could be your suppliers who will provide products or services to you; or it could even be NGOs, think tanks, or peer organisations from the public sector, who collaborate, partner, or provide expertise or advice to you. This analysis should give you insight

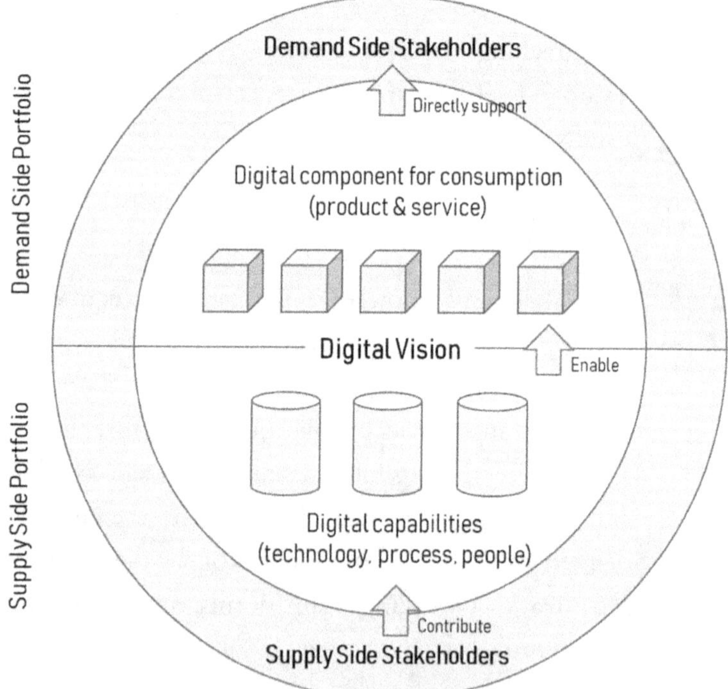

Figure 3 Mapping Digital Components & Capabilities to Stakeholders

into which stakeholders would be your better choice of partnership in delivering your vision. Thus, it is worth your time developing a more tailored narrative to align their objectives with yours, secure their buy-in, and contribute to your cause.

Step 3: Articulating the value of the digital vision for your stakeholders

By now, you should have defined a comprehensive narrative of what your digital vision is about and how it is relevant to your network of stakeholders. The next step is to help each group of your stakeholders better understand why your digital vision **matters** to them. You need to articulate the tangible and intangible values that they can realistically expect to receive after the realisation of the vision. You should try to quantify those values and the degree of changes compared with the status quo and the expected timeframe that they would be achieved. In other words, you should make those expected values as SMART (Specific, Measurable, Achievable, Relevant, Time-bound) as possible. For example, "reducing the processing time of allowance application by 30% for all disabled applicants in 6 months", or "providing teleconsultation services to all follow-up patients in 3 years". You may already notice that these are essentially the expected business outcome, and in turn, the measurement of success of your digital vision. Therefore, when you define these values, they should also be aligned with any overall organisational targets that the business has set.

To make your points more impactful to your stakeholders,

you may consider visualising how their day-to-day life will be different after the realisation of the digital vision. Starting with identifying a scenario that will resonate the most with the stakeholder concerned, while simultaneously demonstrating the positive changes resulting from the vision. Then, under that scenario, describe what and how the existing problems of the stakeholder will be addressed via a story-telling approach. Use lots of visual aids, such as system mock-ups, accompanied by suitable presentation techniques, such as videos or role-playing, to let your target stakeholder groups see and feel how their life will be changed for the better after implementing your digital vision.

For your stakeholders at the supply side, especially your own IT frontline staff, apart from visualising the changes they will face and the outcome or values they are expected to receive, you also need to emphasise how they will contribute to the realisation of the digital vision. In other words, you need to provide a clear answer to the following four questions:

1. What is the overall direction of the IT organisation? Where is the "IT ship" heading?
2. Which parts of the technology components or capabilities of the demand and supply side portfolios will each team own and focus on?
3. Specifically, what is the place of each rank and specialty of your IT staff and other supply-side partners in the overall digital vision?
4. What is the "end state" of my team and myself after the digital transformation?

The ultimate target of this step is to develop the communication packages for each of your key stakeholders to entice them on board, and deliver them at the right platform with the most appropriate format and approach.

Why Do We Need the Hassle?

You may wonder, "what's the point of meticulously analysing each of the stakeholders and tailoring the narratives for them? Wouldn't I be better off putting all these efforts into implementing the vision itself instead?" For public sector's CIOs like you, there are at least two reasons to invest your time in this. Firstly, as mentioned earlier, there are usually many more stakeholder groups in the public sector that could influence or impact the success of your digital strategy. Understanding their relevance and potential reaction to your vision will let you better plan and prepare for their response. Secondly, to uphold accountability and transparency of public sector organisations, there are many more committees, forums and groups that you need to engage to communicate your digital transformation vision than their private sector counterparts. Every one of these groups can have vastly different perspectives and concerns and may support or reject your digital vision for different, or even conflicting, reasons. Therefore, public sector CIOs need to spend more effort in creating a "winning narrative" to sell your vision and secure their buy-in.

The Narrative for Long-term Investment

For more complex technology investments (such as system or architecture refactoring, revamp of infrastructure or systems for core business operations, or large-scale adoption of new and even emerging technology), not only they typically impact multiple areas of technological, but may also involve substantial business process changes, while being expected to take longer to realise any observable business value.

For example, in your digital vision, you will deploy a corporate-wide real-time people flow and asset management platform in dozens of buildings via large-scale implementation of smart sensors and Internet-of-Things (IoT) devices. This will require investment in edge computing and connectivity infrastructure (such as 5G network) for those buildings. To effectively support such a wide variety of devices provided by different suppliers, a corporate-wide technology IoT standard will need to be defined. In addition, data analytics platforms and data visualisation will be essential in extracting business insight from the massive amount of real-time data collected from those IoT devices. This could easily be a multi-million-dollar, multi-year undertaking.

In this case, when you apply the demand-supply narrative framework mentioned above, you need to help your stakeholders to see the big picture and look further into the future, and help them justify the long-term transformation investment and effort with the long-term business value.

In general, your objective is to convince your stakeholders

that your digital vision will address major chronic challenges or risks, or help capture emerging strategic opportunities. You should first describe any short-term quick fixes already in plan, while at the same time emphasise why these will not be a sustainable approach in the long run. These can be justified by reviewing the long term quantitative trends (e.g. growth of service demand, increase in endpoint devices, growth in data, growth in applications and system complexity etc.) as well as qualitative ones (e.g. emerging disruptive societal and political factors that could lead to an exponential increase or decrease beyond the current trend of organic growth, an emerging technology that has the potential of transforming the business model etc.). Industry benchmarking and professional research services, as well as your industry peer network, could give you invaluable insight and help you validate any hypotheses you formed.

Next, based on the trends above, you should then visualise for your stakeholder group the worst-case scenario that might happen to **them** if nothing fundamental and transformative is to be done to address these long-term opportunities or challenges. Of course, this is only a hypothesised scenario. However, you still need to tell a compelling story that is time-specific (e.g. "within 5 years, this will likely happen to you"), and highlights not only the impact to the organisation, but also the impact on the stakeholder personally.

After that, describe how your digital transformation vision can help them avert the worst-case scenario. You can do it by connecting the demand side portfolio with the supply side portfolio, similar to what we discussed earlier. However, given the scale and complexity of the long-term transformation you are proposing, the connection between the demand side components and the supply side capabilities is likely to be complex, with intercorrelations and interdependencies challenging to explain to your stakeholders. One way to deal with this issue is to organise these components into several sub-portfolios based on main target stakeholders, related business outcomes, or other common themes. You can then highlight the parts that are the most relevant and impactful to your target stakeholder groups. You also need to highlight the estimated time and effort it will take to have the prerequisite components and capabilities ready for the stakeholder to see, touch, use and extract benefits from the result of your digital transformation.

The ultimate target of this whole exercise is to build a "burning platform", i.e. an imminent case for the change, to convince your stakeholders that it is justifiable for the organisation to commit effort for a certain period to seize the opportunity or to avert a crisis in the future, and there is no better time to start doing this than right now.

By formulating a convincing narrative, you are also helping your public sector stakeholders defend the case on your and your organisation's behalf: as this kind of digital vision takes longer to realise its ultimate business value than conventional IT initiatives, it will often span across multiple cycles of governance reporting. This could pose a challenge to your business executives from the public organisation, as, over time, they will find it more and more difficult to defend the investment on the transformation against potential criticism from external governance bodies, watchdogs, legislatures, or the general public, if they have no visible outcome to report for months. Therefore, you need to strategically plan your transformation roadmap with a defined timeline and milestones for interim and final deliverables, and prioritise your initiatives so that, from time to time, you will be able to deliver some "low hanging fruits" with outcomes that have higher visibility. Ideally, you should space out the delivery of these initiatives so that your business executives will be able to report new, visible outcomes in every instance of governance reporting. That way, you can help sustain these stakeholders' continuous support.

Effectively communicating your vision and securing your stakeholders' buy-in is an essential step for its realisation. Next, you will need to make it happen. In the next chapter, we will discuss an important part of digital transformation: the transformation of your own IT organisation.

3

Transforming Your Team

Realising your digital vision requires more than new technology. For sure, technology is a crucial enabler of your digital vision. Still, at the end of the day, digital transformation is about the transformation of people and the culture of your organisation by changing the ways of working and mindset of your staff to deliver new value and cope with challenges. It is, however, one of the most challenging parts of your digital transformation journey.

Actions Are Louder Than Words

A few months ago, I had a good chat with a friend from the education sector. She loved to teach and found her career satisfying. She was also a caring mother of two lovely young kids. She was understandably busy, but she also found her career and personal life fulfilling and meaningful.

But then, the COVID-19 pandemic came. With the sudden shift from tradition to online working and teaching, my friend found it hard to cope with the new practice in such a short amount of time. Worse yet, she also needed to take care of her two kids, who were home-bound and needed her support for their own online classes as well. She felt anxious under the tremendous stress but felt helpless to the situation. After over a year, she was close to a mental breakdown, and she did not know what she should do.

"Well...could you change your job?" I asked her, but she just replied, "no, it's too difficult to find another job, especially during the pandemic."

"Could you perform some other non-teaching role for a while?" "That's just impossible."

"Then maybe you could take a week or two off from work?" "No way. And there is nowhere to travel to these days, right? I'll still be stuck at home tutoring my kids!"

"Perhaps you could get someone to take care of your kids while you are at work?" "No, my husband needed to work as well."

"Maybe…you could at least try to make some small changes to your daily routine. Take up a new hobby, or learn some new skills? Sometimes, changing your habits might help to change your mood and perspective." "No, I don't have time for new stuff, and I'm usually too exhausted to do that after a hard day's work and household chores.…"

Not that she had not tried anything, though. She read lots of self-help books to make herself think more positively. She also sought counselling, but none of these seemed to help much either. Unfortunately, she was more or less stuck at where she was. The truth is, when it comes to making any transformation to your life, actions are a thousand times stronger than words; changes in environments and personal behaviours, albeit small as they are, go a much longer way than any advice or texts.

The same principle applies to the transformation of your organisation. Changing your organisation by inspirational speech would not take you far. Instead, you need to consciously induce structural and behavioural changes at both the team level and the individual level to make fundamental transformation happen.

Making Structural Changes

The main objective of making a structural change to the organisation is to realign the role and responsibilities, resources and skills, and the power and leadership of your teams to achieve the new strategic direction of your organisation. In other words, you restructure your organisation so that the right people and groups will be given the proper role, authority and resources to implement what you have envisioned to achieve and that they can interact and cooperate most effectively.

Therefore, you must be clear about why you want to reorganise your IT team, and what outcome you are looking for after restructuring it. Some common reasons include:

- **Improving focus on business objectives**: a shift of

business focus or a significant structural change of your business counterparts may require you to restructure your IT team so that each section (especially the "business-facing" ones like business relationship management and product teams) are organised around each of the strategic business objective, or each of the major stakeholder groups, to ensure they are more accessible to the corresponding business units, and easier for them to align their KPIs with the related business outcome.

- **Breaking the team silos**: for more traditional organisations where being agile is yet to be a norm, team silo is a common phenomenon. Each specialised team tends to work independently without much information exchange or communication with other groups in the organisation. This will create problems for your IT organisation, as they will find it challenging to have a holistic and unified view of the stakeholders' needs and come up with consistent and coordinated actions in responding to those needs. Being silo also means that your team will have a tough time embracing DevOps, which requires a highly collaborative team culture. Reorganising the team (such as changing the team size and the team specialty mix) could be one of the ways to break down the silos.

- **Enhancing team efficiency and performance**: sometimes, you reorganise simply because the teams are not performing up to standard. Changing the team leadership, splitting oversized teams, reducing the level of reporting, or reducing the number of direct reports of your managers may help reduce inefficiency and thus improve the performance of your IT organisation.

- **Cultivating skills and leadership**: to facilitate the development of specific strategic skill domains (such as artificial intelligence, quality assurance, enterprise architecture etc.), you may want to consolidate corresponding staff under the same structure. This will give them more opportunities to interact with peers of the same specialty and further develop their skills. With a defined team and leadership for a particular skill domain, it will also be easier for them to secure training resources and tailor career progression opportunities specific to that speciality. This will, in turn, elevate their professional prestige and thus help retain the internal talents and attract external ones.

No matter what the reasons are, changing the organisation and its people is never easy. Generally, the larger the organisation and the more "fixate" the organisation, the harder it is for it to be transformed. Public sector organisations are often large and, partly due to their nature of risk avoidance, more rigid in terms of organisational structure. As such, you will find it particularly challenging to reorganise your team than your commercial counterparts. It is therefore vital for you to recognise your options for change. Some factors you may need to consider include:

- Who can be the new leaders of each team, and what kind of leadership style would you like them to display?
- What is the skill mix of each team?
- What type of organisational structure should you

choose?

- What is the desired team size, and would that create an imbalance of power among teams?
- Are there any potential major conflicts in culture and style in the new team mix?

While directly changing the organisational hierarchy is a common approach for organisational transformation, this is not your only option. For functions such as IT service operation, if they have well-defined roles and responsibilities that existing skills and human resources can fully support, and, most importantly, have clear and relatively unambiguous targets and output, then a direct change of reporting lines and "real" team structure is a viable choice. However, for less certain areas where services are relatively new to your organisation, and especially those that require new skills and extensive cross-team collaboration, any direct change of reporting lines and formation of a new hierarchical team may not be your best move, as it could be seen as too risky or impractical. Instead, you may consider making use of virtual organisations.

Virtual Organisation

A virtual organisation is formed by a group of talents from different departments, disciplines, ranks, and geographic locations, within or even outside your organisations, to serve and contribute to a set of defined objectives (such as providing technical domain advice and cultivating professionals on a particular domain, or supporting a strategic business direction that any existing functional departments do not yet cover). The members of a virtual organisation are usually drawn from different functional teams of the organisations and report to other managers, but, at the same time, retain their current reporting line and role in their functional units. Some examples of virtual organisations include Communities of Practice (CoP), Centres of Excellence (CoE), and Competency Centres (CC).

Virtual organisations are a bit akin to project teams. However, while a project team is usually formed for achieving a one-off target (such as developing a new product) and has a finite lifetime (it will be disbanded once the project is completed or terminated), a virtual organisation often does not have a defined completion timeframe, and they often serve a more sustained organisational-wide mission. They are also different from committees or task forces, as they do not necessarily have a defined set of deliverables to produce, nor are they meant to be part of the governance bodies. They are, in fact, closer to traditional functional teams in terms of their target outcome.

Since no change in reporting line is needed, and generally no change to members' current role in their function teams, the formation of virtual organisations will have relatively minor disruption to your team as they do not have significant implications to resources or change management. Virtual organisations also have less formality in terms of administration, and are relatively easy to establish, reorganise or disband. Therefore, they can be seen as a lower risk approach that helps transform your team. On the other hand, their informal and "virtual" nature does possess another risk, especially at public sector organisations. Since virtual organisations are not recognised as part of your formal establishment, they will find it more difficult than functional teams to secure the funding and resources they need to advance their mission. Over time, their work may be deprioritised in terms of resources and executive support, even by the members themselves when competing priorities occur. Eventually, the virtual organisations may risk being disbanded or degrading into a status of a mere "interest group". To ensure the sustainability of your virtual organisations so that they can continuously contribute to your digital vision, you should ensure the following elements are in place:

1. **Clearly defined executive ownership**: while there may not be a team manager in the traditional sense for your virtual organisation, you should still need to assign one of your senior leaders to "own" it. This goes beyond being a "sponsor" - the designated senior leader will be accountable to the success or failure of the virtual organisation, and is reflected as part of their personal performance assessment. That way, you will at least have one senior member in your team whose objectives are aligned with that of your virtual organisation.

2. **High visibility to executives**: you need to ensure the work and achievement of your virtual organisation is visible to the IT and even business executives. You should provide a platform for them to demonstrate their value and how it connects with the overall digital transformation vision. This will help the virtual organisation stay relevant in the executives' eyes, thus

keeping their interest and support.

3. **Clear mission statement**: traditional functional teams in a public organisation seldom get challenged once its establishment was approved by a proper governance process and secured funding. On the contrary, you will find virtual organisations often get questioned about their existence, especially when they are not performing up to the stakeholders' expectations or when conflicts emerge with other corporate priorities. Therefore, you need to define a clear mission statement (or even a set of terms of reference) for your virtual organisation, which articulates the reason for their existence, and how it aligns with the overall organisational strategy. This also helps the virtual organisation members to prioritise and focus on what truly matters to the realisation of your digital vision.

4. **Core team**: as most of the members in your virtual organisation contribute on a part-time basis on top of their day-to-day duties, and in some cases, there may even be members outside of your corporate, you need to have a few core team members who will be able to dedicate a majority of their time to the virtual organisation to "keep the ball rolling", and provide day-to-day administration and support to the whole virtual organisation. This is essential to ensure that the initiatives carried out by the virtual organisation will be followed through and that the outcome is properly monitored. As such, you may need to negotiate with your leadership team to relieve the identified core team members (ideally from the functional team of the senior leader who has accountability to the virtual

organisation) from some of their existing responsibilities to free up their time for supporting the virtual organisation.

5. **Regular checkpoints and KPIs**: while virtual organisations may not have a defined end date or final deliverables, it is still important to have regular checkpoints to review the course of your virtual organisation and determine whether it still serves the mission and the overall digital transformation goals as intended. It also provides an opportunity for you and your team to recognise and celebrate any achievements they have made to keep the momentum. Because of this, it would be helpful to devise a simple set of key performance indicators (KPIs) to measure its performance based on its outcome.

Sometimes, a virtual organisation can be a temporary structure. It is expected to gradually evolve into a formal functional team once its value is proven and its operation becomes more mature. For example, if you would like to start exploring the potential application of AI in your organisation and developing experienced in-house AI engineers from scratch, you may consider setting up an AI virtual organisation first. Over time, when the virtual organisation gained more solid experience in AI development, began to cultivate an experienced pool of AI engineers, and even delivered pilot proofs-of-concept or projects that have applied to the real-life business operation, and, most importantly, you started to foresee a continuous business demand to provide on-going AI services and products, you may consider starting the process of transforming it into a formal functional team, with its own dedicated headcount and budget. However, this does not necessarily mean that you need to disband the virtual organisation, as you would likely want to maintain the cross-discipline network you have cultivated. Instead, you may review the mission of the virtual organisation and reposition it as an advisory body to the newly established AI functional team.

For other virtual organisations that highly rely on cross-team collaboration, it is more suitable for them to stay as virtual permanently that complement the hierarchical organisational structure. For example, virtual organisations for driving corporate innovation often rely on collaboration across multiple business units and even external institutions to spearhead innovation initiatives. They also constantly require talents from different specialties and product lines to provide more comprehensive, end-to-end innovation support. The way of operations, outputs and performance metrics are also significantly different from other functional teams. Given these, it would be counter-productive to turn them into traditional hierarchical teams. Instead, they should be kept as virtual to better leverage the flexibility and support from leaders of multiple IT departments and business units.

Pace of Transformation

There is no hard and fast rule to determine the pace of your organisational transformation. Whether to implement the change by phase or in a "big bang" manner, in general, you need to consider several factors, including:

- **Size of the organisation**: the larger or more dispersed the organisation, the more time will generally be needed to communicate and manage staff's expectations, and thus likely to transform at a slower pace.

- **Business criticality**: the more business-critical the function, the higher the risk during transformation due to potential service disruption, and thus buffer and redundancy will need to be built into the plan, which in turn will take more time to transform.

- **Type of transformation**: in general, the more disruptive the transformation approach, the higher the risk you may need to mitigate, and thus you may need to take a slower pace. For example, reorganising the hierarchical structure of functional teams is apparently riskier and should take a longer time than setting up a new virtual organisation.

- **Potential benefits**: while previous factors concern the risk of transformation, benefit brought by transformation is also a factor that determines the pace of change. For example, the benefit of consolidating all existing IT system support functions to form a centralised IT operation centre will only be apparent when at least all core system support staff are reshuffled and centralised. In this case, there is no point in migrating them over a long time, and a big bang approach will be a more sensible option.

Planned Flexibility in Organisational Transformation

Remember this: the reason you transform the organisational structure is to realign it with your digital transformation vision based on your organisation's current state and the external environment. Since both factors are bound to change over time, it only makes sense that the course of your organisational transformation will need to be changed as well. Therefore, you need to build in "planned flexibility" to your transformation plan. From time to time during your transformation journey, you must review and reflect on whether the current course of organisation transformation is still leading your organisation towards your digital vision. You need to examine the outcome and performance of your team, as well as any changes in the external environment, stakeholders' expectations and priorities. If you believe that the current organisational structure can no longer support you achieve your digital vision, you must not hesitate to make changes again.

Take the experience of one of my clients as an example: their IT organisation had been structured around different IT systems since its establishment. Each team was the product of organic growth from the development project team of the application or platform they were commissioned to build: when the project was completed, instead of disbanding the team, they were retained and took up the responsibility of operating and maintaining their systems by adding support staff to their team. This helped retain the business domain knowledge and in-depth system know-how, and the teams generally had strong ownership towards their own systems. However, the downside was that it created very strong team silos, which resulted in a lack of inter-team communications and cohesion and finger-pointing during incidents. Also, as staff of different IT specialties were scattered in different teams, and redeployment between teams was rare, there were few opportunities to develop their skills further. As time went by, such a team structure could no longer support the growing and more complex IT portfolio. The IT systems and services became less reliable and less responsive to business demand.

To implement the corporate digital transformation vision, their CIO saw an urgent need to modernise and specialise the skills of his 1000-staff-strong IT team in order to improve the quality of IT operations, as well as their agility in fulfilling business demand. So a major structural change was implemented to reorganise the IT staff by functional specialty (e.g. development, quality assurance, deployment and operations etc.) instead of by system / project. This was the most significant organisational transformation initiative the IT team had ever seen, and it took over two years to fully implement. About a year after its successful implementation, it saw significant improvement to system availability and reliability and agility in new feature delivery and service provision. It was also able to develop teams of domain experts in various technology areas to support the digital transformation vision.

However, another problem had started to emerge. While the operations and support capability had been significantly improved, the teams seemed overly focused on their own technical functions. They lacked a holistic view of their IT products. While they were now able to deliver quality deliverables with agility, they sometimes found it difficult to fully grasp a holistic picture of the stakeholders' longer-term needs, and were unable to provide an IT product roadmap that aligned with the strategic development of the business. Their CIO recognised that the direction of organisational transformation had to be fine-tuned to meet these emerging challenges, and was not hesitant to change the course by re-designing the development team from technical-centric to product-centric, and emphasising the need for collaboration between development, testing, deployment and operations. Since the IT leadership team had all acknowledged the emerging challenge they were facing, it was relatively easy to secure their buy-in. In addition, the previous round of transformation introduced several virtual organisations that helped break the team silo and encouraged cross-team exchange and cooperation. This allowed greater flexibility and less resistance to any future change.

From the above example, you will see that there are no one-size-fits-all transformation solutions for your organisation that could stay relevant and effective forever. Instead, transformation is often a continuous journey that must be ready to make adjustments for the best interest of your organisation and the realisation of the digital vision. While you need to keep an eye on any significant change in the environment that may urge you to fine-tune the transformation direction, you also need to balance the frequency of change and the stability and morale of your team. Generally, a quarterly or even yearly review would be more appropriate than, say, backtracking and setting a new course every month. Also, if possible, you should wait after the core transformation actions are implemented, and let the team perform for a while to observe its outcome before making any judgement. You should also factor in "planned flexibility" in your change communication to your staff, such as defining key indicators for success, defining critical events that would become a showstopper to the transformation, and outlining any fallback plan to manage your staff's expectation.

Changing People's Behaviour

As mentioned earlier in this chapter, structural change should go hand-in-hand with behavioural changes to make real people transformation. As a new structure often comes with new roles and responsibilities for teams and individual staff, you need to make it clear to your staff about the expected changes in process, daily practice, and norms for interactions between teams or individuals. These are all important to ensure that your organisation will perform as expected and reap the most benefit out of the new structure.

Changing the ways of working and behaviours of your staff needs tactful planning and communication and flexible yet determined execution. Otherwise, after a few months, it will quickly leave you with slogans and motivational posters that nobody cares about, while nothing substantial is changed. The process for leading change by the famous master of change management, Dr. John Kotter, gives us invaluable insight in planning your approach in cultivating the behavioural and cultural shifts required for your digital transformation:

Step 1: Creating Urgency

Your first order of business is to make yourself clear why you need the change in the first place, and why it has to be now. In other words, you need to create the "burning platform" for behavioural changes. It is not enough to think of the urgency from the organisational perspective; you also need to be empathetic and think from the viewpoint of all impacted stakeholders, such as your frontline staff, your IT leadership team, and even your business counterparts. Similar to what we have discussed in Chapter 2 about communicating the digital vision, you also need to form the change narratives for these stakeholders by answering two fundamental questions:

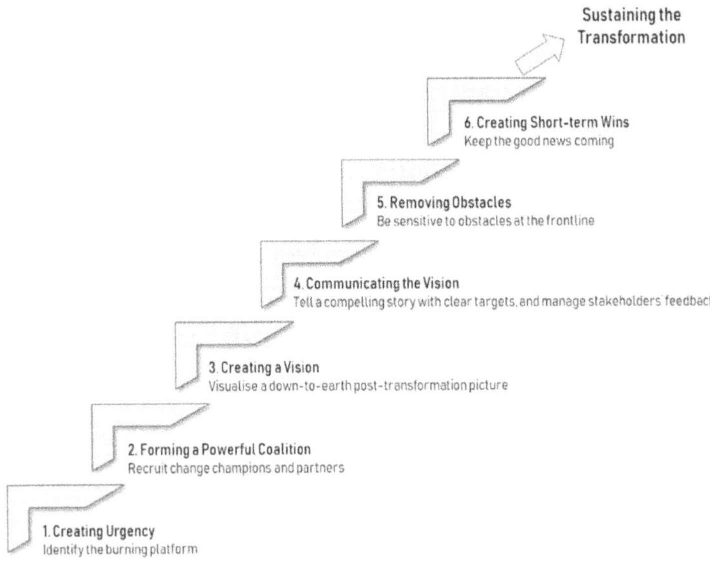

Figure 4 Approach to Changing Staff's Behavisour

"What's in it for me?" and "How will I suffer if the proposed change does not take place?".

Step 2: Forming a Powerful Coalition

After that, you need to have company to begin your change journey. Internally, you need to identify and recruit change champions from your team to be your advocates of change and trusted partners that provide feedback on what their peers think. It is crucial to select champions from all ranks of your staff: senior management and line managers who will lead and implement the many change initiatives, and frontline staff who will be able to provide suggestions and concerns from the daily operation that you, as a CIO, may never be able to have known or thought about. Apart from your IT team, it is also desirable to recruit business executives or other suitable external stakeholders to be your change "partners" or "sponsors", especially if you foresee that the shift in practice will affect these stakeholders somehow.

Step 3: Creating the Vision

Next, you need to work with your change coalition to construct the vision of change. Apart from the objectives and roadmap of the initiatives, more importantly, you need to visualise a simple, down-to-earth picture of post-transformation for each of the stakeholder groups. One way to do it is to compose the "a day of your work after transformation" story, which describes, from an individual, first-person perspective, how their daily work life from dust to dawn will be different from now for a particular stakeholder group. The story should highlight scenarios that are the prime targets of change so that your stakeholders will be able to, from their viewpoint, realise and virtually experience the expected change to their practice and behaviour after the transformation. The vision also serves a key function, especially to your frontline staff, that they are all contributing to the bigger vision of digital transformation, not just "an insignificant gear in the huge corporate machine".

Step 4: Communicating the Vision

The next step is to communicate the change vision to your stakeholders. You should be creative in choosing the most effective communication tools that are best suited for your organisation. A few approaches my clients have used include company blog and vlog (video blog) posts, executive and staff interviews, town hall meetings, role play and micro movies. Apart from painting the beautiful vision, you also need to set clear and visible targets as "beacons of success". For example, suppose you want to introduce new ways of working via a digital workplace platform. In that case, you should define, upon successful transformation, the percentage of meetings conducted virtually rather than in person, how much the consumption of paper will go down, etc.

Effective communication is always a bi-directional process: while you want to promulgate your change vision to your staff, your staff also wants to voice their feedback, concerns, suggestions or grievances. As a change leader, you should be attentive to your team's voice, as this not only builds lasting trust with your staff, their inputs also help you to optimise the change direction and approach. Nonetheless, sometimes you may find that your staff's feedback could be a two-edged sword. While candid and constructive feedback can serve as the fuel of your transformation effort, you may also be worried about the impact on staff morale and confidence if negative sentiments and comments - be they reflect the truth or not - are not handled properly. Therefore, you need a strategy to manage staff feedback in a tactful manner that would enhance the transparency and effectiveness of your cause while minimising any adverse effect on staff's morale and credibility. Generally, you will likely face five types of attitude and reaction from your team:

1. **Vocal supporters**: this group of staff demonstrates strong support to your change direction and approach. They are the ones who are completely aligned with your vision, who have strong buy-in to your transformation goals, and who will likely benefit the most from the transformation. They are your best candidates for being the evangelists of your

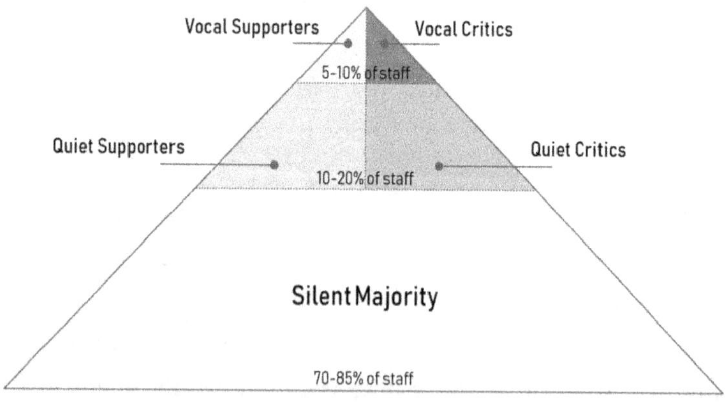

Figure 5 Types of Staff's Reaction to Change

transformation vision.

2. **Silent supporters**: these are the ones who also support your change in general but are less vocal in showing this to their peers. They generally agree with the need to change and the overall direction while potentially having different perspectives and minor concerns in the detailed change implementation approach. However, they are likely to share their opinions and suggestions if engaged.

3. **Silent critics**: this group of staff is the opposite of the "silent supporters", whose buy-in to change is yet to be secured, and still have significant doubts about the transformation. However, out of fear, apathy or other reasons, they usually would keep their opinions to themselves and are unlikely to actively sabotage your change effort, though you should also not count on them to provide meaningful support to your cause.

4. **Vocal critics**: they are the ones whom you may dread dealing with. Not only that they vehemently disagree with the transformation, they also make sure that their peers know about it. It is often the case that they perceive the transformation to be in deep conflict with their own interest and thus see it as a threat. If not managed promptly and appropriately, they will likely undermine your change effort.

5. **Silent majority**: as its name implies, they constitute most of your staff (typically over 70 to 80 per cent), and usually have no strong opinion towards the change. Either they are the passive ones in this context, who will either "tell and do" or, if they perceive the change initiative under significant challenge, may "wait

and see".

Identifying the above staff groups in your organisation will help formulate your strategic communication approach. You may refer to the following principles:

1. For vocal supporters, convert them into your core change agents, and through them, spread the word of mouth of transformation to their peers. They could help grow your base of support among the silent majority.

2. For both the quiet supporters and quiet critics, you need to understand their minds. Create a safe environment to encourage them to express their views and concerns to you. That way opens the door for you to change their mind and provides opportunities for you to realise what may have gone wrong with your change approach and thus fine-tune your change approach and tactics. This also applies to all your staff - by establishing a safe channel for your team to express their view privately without fear of retribution, they will likely become more engaged in the transformation.

3. For the vocal critics, you should actively engage them if possible and discuss with them privately. Your objective is to let them open their heart to you. As long as you can convince them enough to not go against the transformation effort, you may already consider this as success. Even if you fail to change their mind, providing them with a channel to fume out their grievance may also help contain their negative

influence on other staff.

4. Regardless of the type of staff you are dealing with, it is important to let them know that their voice will be heard, although this does not mean that their views will be taken at their face value, nor that they must be right. You, as the leader, should digest their words and discover the concern behind it

5. No matter the comments you receive from staff are positive or negative, it is generally a good idea to let the rest of your staff know about them to enhance transparency. However, when sharing these comments (especially for criticism), you should paraphrase them and filter out unnecessary sentimental wordings or sensitive content, and always be prepared to provide your own response.

Step 5: Removing Obstacles

During the implementation of change, you are bound to face barriers coming from within or beyond your organisation. However, many of these obstacles would not be evident to you, as they usually emerge from the daily operation of your frontline. This is where a strong change core team and effective communication come into play, which will let you be aware of these obstacles as early as possible. To tackle these challenges, you should be a servant leader who focuses on removing the barriers for your team, so that they can continue to work under the new paradigm without significant issues. You should also be sensitive to the grievance, especially from your frontline, and propose fine-tuning and support and recognition to your change champions.

Step 6: Creating Short-term Wins

While people transformation often takes a long time to realise its ultimate vision fully, you should still aim to achieve visible achievement or improvement in the short run, such as KPI improvement in team performance. While promulgating the good news is important, you should also acknowledge any challenges and the actions you will take to address them. That way, you will be able to sustain the confidence of staff and the momentum of change.

An organisational transformation strategy that combines effective structural and behavioural changes will be one of your most potent weapons for realising your digital vision. Next, we will discuss another essential element for doing digital right, but tough to implement in public sector organisations: innovation.

4

Creating Safe Space for Innovation

Innovation is the driver of transformation and change for the organisation. However, not every organisation is ready for this. Innovation is even more scarce among the public sector, where prudence and governance often trump agility and innovation. Public sector organisations are often reluctant to accept new technology and ways of working, and are seemingly obsessed with bureaucratic procedure and governance. As discussed in Chapter 1, there are many reasons behind this culture: they often carry out mission-critical operations that can't risk failure, especially for life-and-death matters such as defence, security and healthcare. They are often too high profile and politically sensitive to fail, given the heavy scrutiny from the public. The decision-makers are also aware that they are spending public money. As such, they are accountable to the public for making responsible use of the resources allocated to them.

Therefore, management from public organisations does not want to be viewed as being careless or even irresponsible in any investment. So there are always multiple layers of panels and committees that scrutinise every new project, investment proposal, and purchase request to ensure that every penny spent is well justified. They are also expected to give immutable target deliverables and delivery timeframe. Once commissioned, they also need to monitor and measure the outcome or the initiatives' return to make sure that the project achieves exactly the deliverables in time and within budget.

This may be good governance from a public administration perspective, but this mindset does not seem to fit the very nature of innovation, where the outcome is less certain, and there is no guarantee of success. The trouble is that many public organisations will apply the same approach of managing regular, "safe" projects to innovation initiatives, and mandate every innovation project must have the same rigid specifications, deliverables and timeline, and the same expectation of successful delivery every time. Unfortunately, such an approach is almost guaranteed to fail, which will likely damage executives' confidence in technology innovation. Over time, with more disappointing results from innovation initiatives, the executives may either shut down innovation entirely or introduce even more monitoring, status reporting, and review panels, hoping that it will not fail again. Either way, innovation is killed.

It was a pity, especially when you realise that the public sector should have been a hotbed for innovation: it often has plenty of workforce, connections and good branding in the industry, problem sets for the most imminent social needs, and in some public agencies, large budgets. As the CIO, you are in a unique position to make innovation work in public organisations and release the power of innovation for the public good.

Framework for Innovation at Public Sector

To this end, a corporate innovation framework is an essential step to start your innovation journey right. There are four aspects that you should consider when designing your framework:

Governance and Oversight

No investment in the public organisation can continue

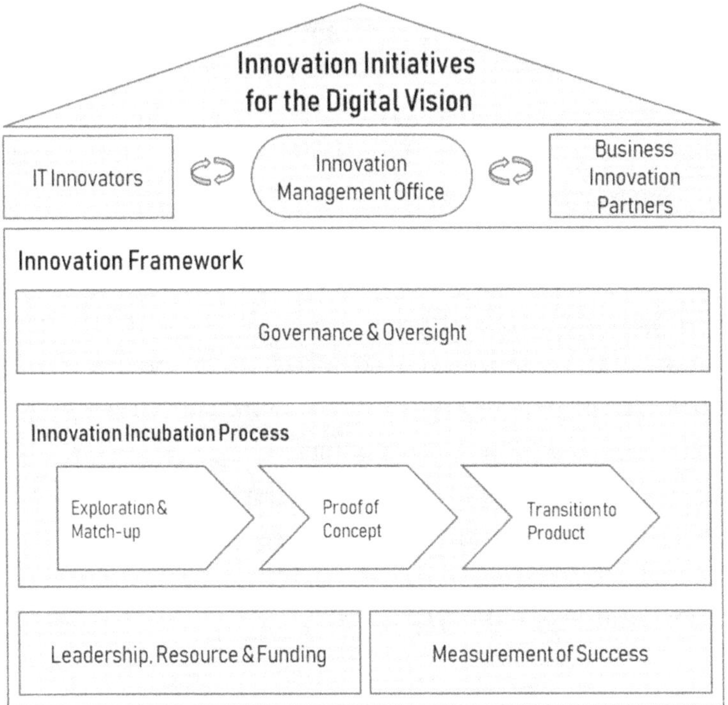

Figure 6   The Innovation Framework

without a certain level of control in place, and innovation is no exception. While elaborated governance structure will become a significant obstacle to innovation, you still need some form of oversight to assure the business executives and other external stakeholders that somebody will be accountable for the investment in innovation.

Given this, when it comes to innovation governance, minimalism is key. Design the governance structure as lean as possible. At the same time, you should ensure that a few top business executives, such as CEO or other C-sites leaders, or even external representatives participate in the innovation governance body. Apart from increasing the credibility of innovation governance in the eyes of different stakeholders, it also allows you to make it a platform to "sell" innovation to the key stakeholders to secure their buy-in and support, at the same time to align the overall innovation priorities with strategic business directions.

You also need to set the right expectation to the members of the governance body when designing the terms of reference: you should position the governance body to be the one to provide strategic direction for innovation, rather than simply monitoring the project progress and budget spending. That way, you can preempt the members to approach their role with the mindset of innovators rather than regulators.

Innovation Incubation Process

This is the most critical component of the whole innovation framework. You need to devise an innovation incubation process that supports realising innovation ideas "from zero to one" and bridging innovation to your conventional product development process to scale up and scale out promising innovations. At the same time, the process should ensure that innovation aligns with the overall digital vision and not to innovate for the sake of innovating. To borrow the saying of IBM, it should ensure the process leads to "innovation that matters" to your organisation and your stakeholders.

Given the above, your innovation process should consist of three major stages:

1. **Exploration and Match-up**: this stage aims at exploring available technology solutions that have the potential of solving your business problem or enabling digital components or capabilities in your vision. During this stage, the team should focus on finding promising technology that matches the needs of your digital vision or other prioritised business challenges. The technology may not be commercially available for large-scale, corporate-wide implementation, but the

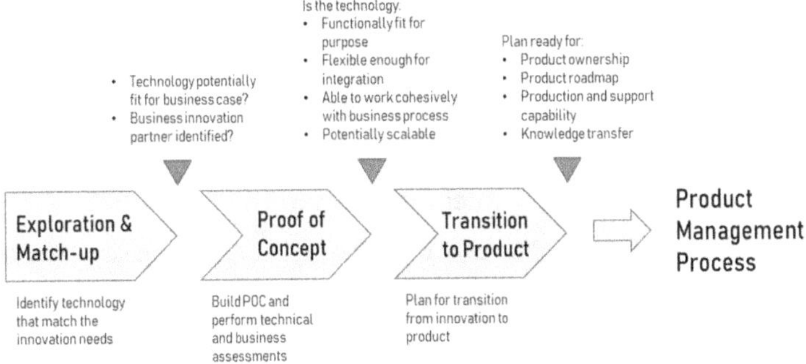

Figure 7   Innovation Incubation Process

technology provider should offer enough flexibility to customise your specific business scenarios, and has the potential for scaled-up delivery in the future. Because of this reason, you should not limit yourself to the conventional technology vendors when sourcing the potential technology; you may approach tech startups, universities or research institutions for emerging technology solutions that are yet readily available in the market. You should leverage your network of innovation ecosystem partners if you have one (we will discuss in the next chapter on building the ecosystem partner network).

2. **Proof of Concept**: once a potential technology is identified, the focus will shift to building proofs-of-concept to prove its technical feasibility. Apart from the functional capability, it would be best to examine the integration flexibility with your existing technology platform and systems and how well the innovation solution will work with the business workflow and process. As such, it is recommended to have identified your business innovation partners at the beginning of this stage to co-develop the proof-of-concept. The objective of this stage is to assess whether the technology can deliver the capability as expected, as well as its potential of scaling out to departmental or corporate-wide implementation in the future.

3. **Transition to Product**: if the result of the assessment at the previous stage shows that the innovation has the potential of scaling up for corporate-wide implementation, you will need to plan for its transition from innovation to proper product development. You

should consider the timeframe and preparation required for production and adoption at a much larger scale of operation. You will need to plan for the production and subsequent support capability for such a large scale of use (especially for solutions that require hardware production), as well as the ownership and roadmap of this new product. You also need to make sure knowledge and lessons learned during the POC stage are captured and transferred from the innovation team to the product team. Once these are determined, the innovation can now be transferred to the new owner of the initiative, and managed by the existing mechanism and governance of the regular project and product management.

You also have to prevent any innovation initiatives from being stuck at a particular stage for a prolonged time and gradually falling into limbo. Between different stages, you need to make sure that there are decision gates and "acceleration" mechanisms for moving things forward and past different stages. It would help if you also designed the exit mechanism at each stage to allow quick abandonment of innovation ideas and initiatives that do not work.

Leadership, Resource and Funding

Since innovation is usually not a standing function of a public sector organisation, you will find it hard to secure resources at its beginning. It is not uncommon for public organisations to assign a manager to take innovation as an additional task. In your framework, you should at least define the role and responsibility of the key person in charge of administering the innovation process. This "innovation manager" or "innovation officer" should be the go-to person to coordinate and execute all technology innovation-related initiatives. If this is not a full-time role in your organisation, you should expect the assignee of this role should spend at least half of their time on innovation-related matters. However, they can be supported by other resources, likely in the form of a virtual organisation formed by staff members with technical and administrative backgrounds.

While it is possible to start your innovation team without dedicated human resources, it is highly recommended to commit to regular dedicated funding for innovation. Regardless of the funding source, you should reserve a funding amount that is neither too large (which may cause concern to the business executives or external stakeholders on something unproven) nor too small (which you cannot practically deliver anything). Not counting salaries, you may aim at, say, no more than 0.5% to 1% of your annual IT operating costs as a start. Also, you should ensure that the funding is recurrent, at least in principle. This is essential to ensure and demonstrate the organisation's long-term commitment to innovation. The purpose of the funding should be primarily for one-off investment such as setting up essential platforms and tools, as well as supporting the implementation of proofs-of-concept. Since the amount of funding is limited, you should avoid capital investment as far as possible to reduce the long-term cost of ownership and retain operational flexibility and agility.

Measurement of Success

As previously mentioned, traditional project metrics cannot be directly applied to innovation initiatives. Therefore, in your framework, you need to define metrics to measure innovation success. The main objective is to assess and demonstrate whether the investment in innovation has led to outcomes that contribute to the digital vision. You do not need an elaborate set of measurements, instead, you may adopt 2 to 4 metrics that focus on:

- The number of new innovation ideas discovered
- The number / percentage of innovation ideas converted into proofs-of-concept
- The number / percentage of proofs-of-concept assessed to be suitable for full implementation
- The number / percentage of staff and ecosystem partners engaged in innovation

Innovation Framework as a Safety Net

Your innovation framework, ultimately, serves as a "safety net" for both the senior executives and external parties, as well as your internal innovators. To the executives, the framework provides a transparent mechanism to give them peace of mind, knowing that the innovation will happen in a setting that they can monitor and control and have a way to pull out if necessary. To your innovators, it provides a safe space to experiment new ideas, knowing that they are not asked to guarantee success. This will allow you to nurture a culture of learning from failure and mistakes in your organisation, which is also beneficial to the realisation of digital transformation.

The framework also introduces concepts and vocabulary new to many public organisations (such as proofs-of-concept, different phases of innovation that precede regular projects). Using a different language and ways of thinking to talk about innovation helps reframe the mindset of all stakeholders towards innovation and free you and them from the restraint of the traditional project mindset.

Getting the Right Innovators

In parallel to setting up the innovation framework, it is equally important to recruit the right people to generate the spark of innovation. As mentioned previously, in organisations that lack a culture of innovation, you as the CIO often are the one best positioned to take the lead as part of digital transformation. It is, therefore, natural for you to recruit the first team of innovators among your own staff.

Let's say you have found a team of passionate engineers to be the pioneers. You provide them with a business problem to solve, allocate them a small budget, and then give them a free hand to innovate. It may work at the start and may even generate promising initial results. However, while the prototype may look technically sophisticated, the business "client" does not see it that way. They do not see the innovation address their day-to-day business problem as promised. They believe that the engineers approached the problem from the wrong perspective, and the prototype would never fit the business workflow and practice. From the business point of view, innovation provides little value to them. This not only disappoints the business stakeholders but is also discouraging to your innovators.

This happened to one of my healthcare sector clients, whose IT innovation team spent a month designing their first innovation prototype for the pharmacy department, which was an IoT-enabled smart drug box device that would automatically remind patients to take their medication. However, the device was too bulky for the patients compared to the traditional pill bottles. At the same time, the dispensers of the pharmacy also found it unappealing, as it solved none of their problems while introducing more work to them, since the device required them to take more steps when refilling drugs comparing to using conventional drug packaging drugs. Needless to say, the prototype went nowhere. However, the team did learn a valuable lesson: IT could not innovate alone, and it was essential to see from the perspective of the target beneficiaries at the very beginning of their innovation journey.

It is therefore important to secure the business or the clients as your innovation partners. To do so, your innovation team should dive deep into different business units and stakeholder groups, talk face to face with the management, the frontline, and the end-users. Your team should be a good listener who is eager to understand the daily business problem, and be a collaborative partner to co-innovative a potential technology solution with the business. Your team also plays the role of technology evangelist, who is passionate about opening the eyes of the business by showing them how the technology can potentially apply to solve similar problems in other organisations or industries. For the first innovation initiative with the business, your team should make your business partner feel comfortable to do this "leap of faith" with them by identifying "low hanging fruit", i.e. something relatively easy and quick to yield visible results that solve the partner's day-to-day problem. As you can see, your innovation team should not only consist of technology geeks, but also communicators and consultants, who can methodically explore the innovation needs of your business, guide them and the technical innovators to co-innovate a solution, and forge trust and partnership between the business and the IT innovation team.

While your team works closely with the business, you as the leader should help direct your team's innovation focus on the big picture of digital vision, and help them prioritise their effort on ideas that are more likely to generate transformative improvement that would create true and lasting impact to the whole organisation.

The Innovation Management Office (IMO)

Given the complexity of driving innovation, you should consider building a virtual team to coordinate innovation. Led by the innovation manager as mentioned above, this virtual team (known as the "Innovation Management Office" (IMO), or simply "Innovation Office") not only provides administrative and project management support, but most importantly plans and coordinates the liaison and engagement with business and other stakeholders. An effective IMO should deliver the following functions:

1. Facilitate and follow up on innovation initiatives, from ideation and technology exploration, to solution brainstorming and delivery of prototype / proof-of-concepts

2. Bridge with the product development team to align between innovation and product / solution roadmap

3. Provide and manage the testing environment and facilitate for technology assessment and proof-of-concept development and trial before deploying or testing at real business operation environment

4. Serve as the single point of contact for the ecosystem, negotiate and form partnerships, and promote innovation to the external partners

5. Promote and educate staff on innovation awareness, and recruit partners for innovation initiatives

Successfully introducing and driving innovation at your organisation will significantly contribute to the technology, people and culture transformations. In fact, enabling innovation is already a remarkable achievement of transformation in itself, and will undoubtedly propel your organisation closer to the desired digital vision.

Sustaining the Transformation

5

Scaling Up Your Innovation

No one can innovate alone. While at the beginning of your innovation journey, you may need to rely on the in-house heavily, often voluntary, innovators (see Chapter 4), it cannot last for long. It is true that in-house innovators are good at leading innovation in its infancy and play a crucial role in cultivating innovation in your organisation. They also have deep local business domain expertise, and may leverage existing networks with business and other stakeholders to promote co-innovation in the enterprise. But after establishing the foundation and building the initial momentum, problems will emerge: after a few successful in-house innovation projects and proven its potential to the business, you may start getting more and more requests from the business to co-innovate with you. Your staff will find it more and more challenging to handle all of those requests, especially when the majority of them may only still be supporting innovation on a part-time basis.

Therefore, as you try to scale up your innovation, you will need more partners beyond your organisation to sustain the innovation journey. Fortunately, the scale and brand of public organisations mean that there are often plenty of partners that would be willing to collaborate with you. Nonetheless, it is essential to know your options and pick the best type of partners for your innovation initiatives.

Finding the Right Innovation Partners

Depending on the nature and maturity of your innovation initiatives, one or more of the following entities could be your potential partners in scaling up your innovation, though each of them has its pros and cons when you work with them:

1. **Technology startups**: local technology startups tend to be small companies that specialise in one to two innovative products. While they are generally more flexible in terms of solution offering, they are often only able to provide point solutions (i.e. solutions that can address only one specific problem). Thus they will more likely oversimplify your complex business challenge into something their product can address. You also need to be mindful of their capability of scaling up and out if, some days later, you want to apply their solution to the whole organisation.

2. **"Big tech" vendors**: these include the big names of technology solution providers. While their solutioning capability and experience are strong and can often provide comprehensive services, their products are usually expensive. They tend to be less accommodating to your request to tailor their solutions for you. You may also need to think long term when engaging with

them for core technology platform or infrastructure provision, as it is easy for you to fall into the vendor lock-up trap. However, it is possible to convert a competent vendor into your strategic partner, who will serve as an integration platform of your innovation efforts.

3. **Academic research institutions**: these include universities and other not-for-profit research institutions. They are generally more innovative and possess more advanced technology, but you need to be mindful of their readiness to translate their research into practical solutions in the short run, as their primary interest will be research publication rather than solving your business problems. Nonetheless, they are generally good long-term strategic partners, in particular for greenfield emerging technology collaboration. However, you and your innovation team may need to deal with arrangements such as funding and intellectual property (IP) rights.

4. **Technology Transfer Offices (TTOs) and applied research institutions**: Nowadays, universities are keen on bringing their research results into the industry through their TTOs. In addition, many governments also set up public-funded or public-subsidized applied research institutions to bridge the academic institutions with the commercial world. They could become your valuable strategic partners, as their objective is better aligned with yours, i.e., applying advanced technology to solve your strategic business challenges. In many jurisdictions, there may even be government subsidies for collaboration projects with these institutions.

Platforms for Reaching Out

As mentioned in the previous chapter, a critical success factor of innovation is to bring in innovation that matters, that is, innovation relevant to your stakeholders and address their pain points. However, your innovation team does have its limitations: they are not at the business frontline, and no matter how hard they try, they will never have the same understanding as their business counterparts; they are also not a research institution, and will never attain the same proficiency as universities or market research firms in terms of the most updated technology solutions available in the ecosystem. Therefore, your innovation team needs to open themselves to the business frontline to understand their problems and the ecosystem to suggest ideas and solutions addressing your business problems. What you need is a comprehensive platform for innovation that connects your team internally to the business and externally to the ecosystem, physically and virtually. The components of this platform include:

1. **External virtual platform**: a web portal that displays the innovation demands or problem sets of your organisation, as well as success stories of innovation. On the other hand, it allows any technology partners or vendors in the ecosystem to submit their solutions. The objective is to attract potential solutions while allowing your potential collaborators to understand your needs better and be aware of the possible outcome of collaborating with your organisations. Note that this is not an electronic platform for Request

For Proposal (RFP). The purpose of this platform is primarily for market research and promotion.

2. **Internal virtual platform**: an intranet web portal for browsing relevant solutions by your staff or other supply-side stakeholders (see Chapter 2), and allowing them to submit their innovation needs and ideas. The platform should be administered by your Innovation Management Office (IMO) to ensure timely follow-up of any idea / need submission from your stakeholders.

3. **Internal physical platform**: this may include cross-departmental think tanks for brainstorming innovative ideas and facilitating cross-domain collaboration. It may also include institutions that promote and educate innovation among your internal business stakeholders.

4. **External physical platform**: physical lab or collaboration workspace, equipped with testing facilities and systems for experimenting with prototyping under a controlled environment before deploying them to a real-life environment for trial. It should also provide areas for demonstrating your business problems and showcasing the result of

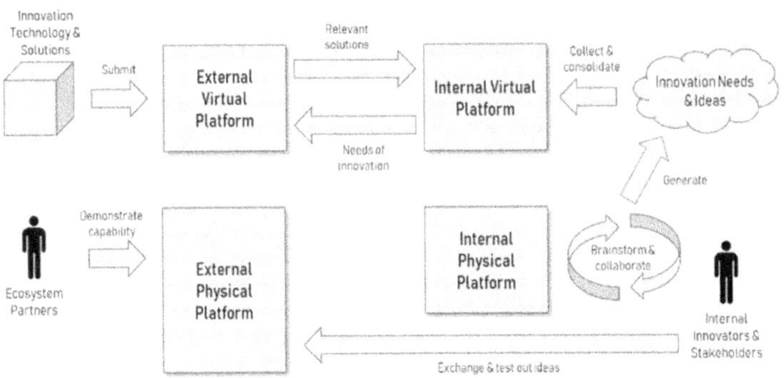

Figure 8 Innovation Platforms

innovation (such as technology prototypes), and communal areas for idea exchange in a more casual setting, and facilitating interaction with external partners.

Other Thoughts on Sustaining Innovation

To sustain innovation in your organisation, you should be aware of the "innovation silo" pitfall: i.e. having numerous point-solutions that could only be applied to a very narrow set of use cases on a small scale. They generally lack any integration capability with any of the existing infrastructure and systems, nor any potential to scale up and scale out for broader rollout. This often happens when many innovation initiatives are carried out without coordination, and lack technology standards or platforms to ensure their integration capability and interoperability with other technologies. Such innovations will likely be able to stay at the proof-of-concept stage forever.

To ensure successful innovation not stay as "innovation" forever, you also need to give them a clear pathway and mechanism to push the high potential innovation through your product and service offering roadmap, scaling out to the whole organisation. Your innovation team needs to closely work with the corresponding product and operation teams to ensure a successful post-innovation transition. They need to, for example, define the assessment criteria and mechanism needed for evaluating and determining which innovation initiatives can be "graduated" to become a full-fledged product, ensure its inclusion into the overall product roadmap via corresponding product management process, and support the planning for development and operation support resource needs.

The most important thing is to demonstrate tangible and visible value from your innovation continuously. You need to measure your innovation with suitable KPIs (see the Innovation Framework in Chapter 4). Not only that, you need to make sure your stakeholders know about the success and lessons learnt. You need to promulgate in every suitable platform in your organisation: from the board and executive meetings, town hall, staff meeting, to videos and blogs. Better yet, showcase your innovation success stories by your business innovation partners instead of just by IT innovators.

The ultimate vision of innovation is that every technology project in the organisation will become an innovation project. In some public organisations, every project proposal must include some aspects of innovation to secure approval. That way, innovation will blend into every part of the organisation, and become part of every staff's language from frontline to executives. Perhaps this will be the best way to sustain innovation in your organisation as well.

6

Sustaining the Internal Change Momentum

You have devised the digital vision for the next several years of your organisation. You made every effort to ensure the overall corporate strategic directions and the digital vision aligned with each other. You articulated its relevance to your stakeholders to the best of your ability. You presented to the board and got their endorsement. You also briefed your own IT staff in the town hall meetings. Everybody was energised and supported it enthusiastically.

However, a few months later, your business stakeholders have already forgotten what you said, and queried about your new strategic technology investment. Your IT staff also seems to have forgotten about the digital vision. The passion was gone, and they started to question why they have to do this new initiative instead of other teams, and started to let day-to-day operation and firefighting overtake the momentum of transformative initiatives you have started a few months ago. It only comes up again, perhaps every year, when you need to report to the board for its progress. No one seemed to care, and they just treated it as another bunch of IT projects. Your digital vision, unfortunately, became another "big idea" that failed to leave the footstep of your office.

Successful transformation is complex, but it is even more challenging to sustain the momentum of change till it is fully realised. It is a sad but common scene in a lot of enterprises to see a lot of pomp and circumstance at the beginning of their transformation journey, only to see it falter over time, where passionate actions turning into routine and irrelevance, dying out "not with a bang, but with a whimper".

No doubt that making your digital vision aligned and relevant is important - we have discussed this in detail in Chapter 2. However, you need to ingrain that vision in their daily life to make it sustainable. To do so, you should make your digital vision into your stakeholder's everyday language.

Making Digital Vision into Everyday's Language

A proper communication approach to "market" your digital vision plays an important role (we have discussed some of these approaches in Chapter 3), but the message itself is equally important. As described in Chapter 2, you need to articulate how your vision relates to your stakeholders, the concrete and actionable implications to each group of your stakeholders, and their expected values. However, to make the realisation of the digital vision part of the daily life of your stakeholders, especially your staff and the business, you would want your stakeholders to own your vision. You should define and let everybody know which department, team or leader will be the owner of a particular portfolio, component or capability of your digital vision, who will lead and be accountable for its successful realisation. Ideally, each of your top IT executives and major IT functional teams should be assigned as the owner of at least one of the portfolio or major components. It would help if you also lobbied the relevant business units and their corresponding business executives to be the "sponsors" of different digital vision components. Sharing the ownership of your digital vision with the business can help you get allies in the organisation during the implementation of your digital vision.

To effectively engage the broader staff group in your IT organisation, you also need to be tactful in the type and depth of your communication content to let them feel relevant. They (especially the frontline IT staff) are more interested in knowing the "how" part of your digital transformation: you should tailor your message to each of your staff groups based on their ranks and roles, and focus on their position, what they will deliver, and the immediate priorities and actions needed from them. On the other hand, you may want to keep the "why and what" (such as new concepts) of your digital transformation as simple as possible, but also as frequent as possible. For example, you may package such kind of information into bite-size contents, and make them as easily accessible as possible via multiple channels, e.g. intranet site, departmental and corporate blog site or video channel, and deliver them as regularly as possible (think weekly electronic newsletters / updates, posters on electronic bulletin boards etc.). To ensure the digital vision is articulated by your IT management in future projects and investments, you may make it mandatory to have a section in their business case that describes how the initiative will contribute to a particular strategic portfolio.

Eventually, you will find that when your staff begin to talk about your digital vision every day, they will be more willing to innovate and take on more ambitious initiatives. They would be more inclined to think that they are empowered to take risks to achieve the strategic initiatives. This could be transformative to the public organisations that traditionally emphasise risk aversion and "following the rules".

Similarly, you also need to sustain the business interest and engagement in the digital transformation journey by regularly updating them of the implementation progress, and any interim benefits realised or lessons learned acquired. Let them talk about their feedback, be it positive or negative. This not only will allow you to fine-tune your course as required, it also makes sure that the digital vision continues to be on the agenda of the senior executives. Therefore, persistence is the key, and such updates will only get more important to you as time goes by.

Applying OKR to Keep the Change Momentum

As discussed in Chapter 3, a crucial part of organisational transformation is to drive behavioural change. However, the traditional "carrots" or "sticks" for behavioural changes, such as promotion (even in title), bonuses and other monetary awards, or demotion and termination, are generally inapplicable to public sector organisations due to regulatory or policy limitations. You will therefore need different tools to incentivise changes. A potentially powerful tool is the "Objective - Key Result" (OKR) goal-setting framework.

OKR is a lightweight approach for setting individual and team objectives, as well as tracking its progress. Since its inception in the 1980s at Intel, it is now widely adopted in many technology enterprises. At Google, for example, each staff will define 3 to 5 OKRs every quarter, with specific and measurable targets to achieve. OKRs are usually created by individual staff upon discussion with their managers. Every OKRs, from the ones by the CEO to those by the most junior engineers, are visible by every staff member to promote transparency and cross-team alignment. The progress of OKRs is evaluated from time to time, and because it is encouraged to set more ambitious goals, it is expected that the OKRs will not be fully met. The average success rate of each OKR is only around 70%. Overall, the OKR framework provides a simple way to let everybody in the organisation know everybody's priorities and progress, simply quantify their target results, encourage staff to take calculated risks, and ensure everyone's priorities align with the organisation's strategic direction.

Given the above characteristics, you may realise that OKR is the ideal tool to drive digital transformation by translating it into concrete and measurable goals. By first defining the key priorities and themes to achieve by the leadership team for the IT organisation in a given timeframe, your team can develop their digital transformation OKRs in a bottom-up manner following these directions, and have their progress tracked and reported from time to time. You and the IT executive team will have a comprehensive picture of the overall transformation progress. Staff are also encouraged to set stretch targets that push them out of their comfort zone, which is suitable for less certain ambitions like digital transformation.

However, the problem is that not many public sector organisations have adopted OKR. Most likely, your organisation already has an established, enterprise-wide staff appraisal system. Therefore, your strategy is to make OKR a tool complementary to the existing performance evaluation system, rather than overlapping (which would be redundant) or overriding (which would be impractical) it. The following principles would be helpful for you to strategically position the adoption of OKR:

1. There are two types of OKRs: the committed OKRs, which are agreed to achieve 100%; and the aspirational OKRs, which are less certain and often stretched targets. You should emphasise the "aspirational" type of OKR instead of "committed" ones to not overlap with the existing project progress reporting or staff performance measurement mechanisms. The key is to let the staff know that it is okay to aim high and take risks.

2. While staff appraisal requires confidentiality, OKR encourages and even mandates transparency. Making everyone's priorities and progress visible to everyone can gradually transform your team culture. It can break

down team silos and force the teams to communicate frequently and collaborate with each other to align their OKRs better.

3. While staff appraisal measures the performance of individual staff, OKR measures the attainment of objectives. The OKR review and reporting process highlight cross-team collaboration and lessons learnt, rather than the success or failure of individual staff. OKR measurement should be as quantifiable as possible, and should be focused on business outcome and impact.

While OKR is a powerful tool, the planning and review processes that accompany OKR are equally vital to its success.

In public sector organisations, where the culture is traditionally more hierarchical, OKRs are often set top-down, i.e. the top management will first set their OKRs, and they will be "cascaded" downwards to their direct reports, who will in turns set their own OKRs based on the ones "descended" from their bosses. For example, suppose their manager has the following OKR: "Increase the number of public service mobile app users by 30%". In that case, their direct reports may define their OKRs by making them more specific to their own roles, like "Rollout xyz features on the app to attract new users". While this ensures strong alignment with the top-level strategic directions, it may inadvertently discourage staff from taking the initiative to achieve the target in their own way, and thus potentially stifle innovation. Therefore, it is desirable to allow OKRs to be set from both top-down and bottom-up, as long as they align with the overall strategic priorities.

For the OKR progress review process, it should be reasonably regular, say monthly or bi-weekly, to make it stay relevant all the time. The whole process should be as lightweight and accessible as possible. Many OKR management tools provide an intuitive approach for every staff member to update the OKR progress in a minute. To allow reporting of OKR progress meaningful to the business, it is recommended to tie each of the OKR to different portfolios or critical components of the digital vision.

Although the outcome of OKR does not have the same "binding" effect on individual staff as the appraisal, it does not mean that it is a "paper tiger": its power lies in its transparency. By making OKR highly visible and permeating your IT organisation's everyday language, you can make your staff know that OKR matters in the organisation. By making OKR part of your staff day to day process and language, you will be able to leverage its power to drive your organisation towards your digital vision.

7

Sustaining External Support

While public sector organisations are not private companies that need to sell their products, they still need marketing. We have already discussed extensively about communicating your vision with your internal business and IT stakeholders in previous chapters. In this final chapter, we will briefly discuss the importance of planning and managing communication with your stakeholders external to your organisation.

Communication to Sustain External Support

As a public sector organisation, external stakeholders, such as the media, other government agencies, the legislature, special interest groups and pressure groups, and the general public, also play a role in making or breaking your digital vision, and their support is also crucial to the eventual success of the digital transformation. Therefore, you need to keep these stakeholders informed and let them feel engaged (albeit the level of information and engagement will be vastly different among these stakeholders, depending on their influence on the digital vision, and the potential impact to them brought by the realisation of the digital vision). You certainly do not require to provide detailed progress reports to every single citizen. Instead, the objective of your communication to these stakeholders is to demonstrate that we are continuously delivering the value that matters to those external stakeholders as well as internal staff, while maintaining transparency, fairness and reasonable oversight of the use of money.

The media and industry conferences are excellent platforms to showcase your success stories of digital transformation. You will find it helpful to work closely with your organisation's media relations or corporate communication team to explore the potential stories that are positive and newsworthy for media coverage. You should also use other platforms, such as professional symposiums, trade shows, or other industry events to promote your stories while exploring and attracting potential collaboration partners from the ecosystem. Assuming no concern on conflict of interest or potentially causing any negative perception from the public, you may also work with advisory firms, research institutions, think tanks and other NGOs to produce case studies based on your journey of transformation.

You may also devise a strategy to handle any negative press due to issues or incidents coming out of the transformation. You would not be able to stop any related negative press, but you can mitigate the impact brought by them. The key is to respond proactively, rapidly and to the point, communicate the incident or problem in layman terms, any effects to your stakeholders, and most importantly, when it will be fixed. Again, it would help if you worked closely with your media liaison team. Your objective is to reassure users that things are under control and act as transparent as possible.

Securing external stakeholders' support may, in turn, enhance your support among internal stakeholders. Showing the support from external media and groups add credibility to your digital vision from the eye of your internal stakeholders, as it, to a certain extent, demonstrates that your digital vision is addressing the needs of their stakeholders as well, which help secure continuous investment and executive support to your transformation effort.

When Digital Has Been Done Right

Every organisation is unique. I may not be able to cover every approach and tactic in this short book for making your digital transformation successful. However, if you start noticing the following changes in your organisation, you should know that you have done the right thing and on the road to realising your digital vision and being "world-class":

1. Your organisation has acknowledged the "burning platform" and the urgency to transform, and realised that digital transformation is a business priority rather than just an IT initiative.
2. Your team understands the need for organisational transformation, and you started to see more and more cross-team communication and collaboration.

3. Both the business and your IT team are getting used to innovation, and see innovation not as a risk, but an essential corporate capability for attaining the digital vision.

4. Your team embraces (or at least gets more comfortable with) transparency. They are also more willing to take calculated risks and take on aspirational targets that are less certain in the outcome.

5. Your IT team is more willing to reach out to the business and other external stakeholders. Your team gained the reputation of knowing the needs and concerns of their stakeholders well, and can think from their perspective.

6. You started to make partners in the ecosystem and no longer innovate alone. The industry recognises your organisation's digital capability - your organisation is being seen as a leader rather than a laggard in technology.

Thank you for reading this till the end. If you have already been planning or implementing the digital transformation in your organisation transformation, I hope this book has inspired you when reflecting on your strategy and approach. If you are still hesitating about starting your digital transformation, I hope this book can give you the push to begin this meaningful journey. Either way, I wish you every success in your digital transformation journey.

REFERENCES

Doerr, J. (2018). Measure What Matters: OKRs - the Simple Idea That Drives 10x Growth. Portfolio Penguin.

Economic Commission for Europe, & Leyden, D. P., Innovation in the Public Sector2–17 (2017). Geneva, Switzerland; United Nations Publications.

Gartner Inc. (2021). Definition of Chief Information Officer (CIO) - Gartner Information Technology Glossary. Gartner. https://www.gartner.com/en/information-technology/glossary/cio-chief-information-officer.

Gray, D., Brown, S., & Macanufo, J. (2010). Gamestorming: A Playbook for Innovators, Rulebreakers, and Changemakers. O'Reilly.

Gray, D., Reid, S., Gray, D., & Boehm, N. (2017, July 23). Empathy Map. Gamestorming. https://gamestorming.com/empathy-map/.

High, P. A. (2009). World Class IT: Why Businesses Succeed When IT Triumphs. Jossey-Bass.

REFERENCES

International Business Machines Corporation. (2015, March 9). Our Approach. https://www.ibm.com/ibm/responsibility/2015/at_a_glance/our_approach.html.

Kotter, J. P. (2012). Leading Change. Harvard Business School Press.

ACKNOWLEDGEMENTS

This book is my first ever writing published for public consumption. Writing this book was an excellent opportunity for me to reflect on what I have learned from my 15 years of consulting practice so far. Looking back, I was humbled and grateful for the many amazing persons in my life who made all of these possible.

Firstly, a heartfelt thanks to my boss, mentor and friend Kevin Cai. He is one of the most influential persons in my career development. I am grateful to have worked with him on some of the most challenging digital transformation initiatives in the public sector. In fact, many of the frameworks and practices mentioned in this book are inspired by my works with Kevin over the past six years.

My thanks to Dr N T Cheung, one of the most visionary digital pioneers I have ever met, for his leadership, inspiration and support. It was my honour to have served in his team.

I would also like to thank Steven Davidson, a veteran business and technology strategist, and my first mentor in the consulting practice. His inspiring wisdom, leadership, and work ethic have demonstrated what a role model consultant and leader should be like.

Thanks to my past and present teams and colleagues from my internal and external consultancy practices. Many of them have since become prominent leaders and entrepreneurs in various industries. Special thanks to Vikas Kharbanda, Yvonne Cheang, Sammie Shum, Vincent Wong, Vincent Fan and Valerie Tse from IBM Hong Kong; Phil Lansley, Dennis Lee, Mavis Wong, Dr Kenny Yuen, Dr C T Lui and Dick Ngan from Hong Kong Hospital Authority.

Thanks to my parents, Jacob and Anna, for their nurturing and unfailing support in every stage of my life.

Thanks to my son, Aloysius, who is the joy of my life and my motivation to work hard.

And most importantly, I thank my wife, Grace, the most important companion in my life. She is always by my side through my peaks and troughs. She supports me all the way, by all means. Whatever little honour that I managed to achieve so far, she totally deserves the credit. Thank you, my dear, for your unconditional love.

ABOUT THE AUTHOR

Raphael Hui is a seasoned IT strategist with vast experience in the public sector. He has advised internal and external clients for over 15 years, including healthcare, transportation, entertainment, financial and public service industries, providing consultation and hands-on support for their digital transformation, organisational change, and technology innovation journeys. He is also the inaugural Head of the Hong Kong Hospital Authority's Institute of Health Information Technology (IHIT). Raphael is a certified Project Management Professional (PMP), and holds a Master degree in Health Services Management (with Valedictorian honour) from the Chinese University of Hong Kong, as well as dual Bachelor degrees of Software Engineering and Information Systems from the University of Hong Kong.

www.ingramcontent.com/pod-product-compliance
Lightning Source LLC
Chambersburg PA
CBHW071643170726
48000CB00023B/829